This Book Belongs To:

____

Your

FAITH

can move

mountains

Matthew 17:20

I Know I Am Loved Because...

I Believe God Will...

I Am Grateful For....

I Give Up The Need To Be Right About....

I Trust And Believe...

Where

God

guides

He provides

Isaiah 58:11

There Is Nothing To Fear Because....

To Achieve My Dreams, I Will....

My Prayer For Today Is....

God Will Make A Way For....

I Can...

With God all things are possible

Matthew 19:26

Evidence of God's Love For Me Includes....

Today, I Ask God To Help Me With....

I Am Grateful I Have Overcome....

I Thank God For....

I Trust That....

Faith

it does not
make things
easier
it makes them
possible

Luke 1:37

I Appreciate....

I Forgive Myself For....

I Prayed & Heard God Say....

My Joy Comes From...

I Forgive Others For....

HIS grace is ENOUGH

2 Corinthians 12:9

I Send Loving Thoughts To....

I Promise Myself That....

I Release....

My Peace Comes From....

Today, I Feel....

Be still
and
KNOW
that I am
GOD
Psalm 46:10

I Ask For The Strength To....

I Fondly Remember....

I Am No Longer Afraid Of....

I Love My....

I Am Becoming....

Every *good*

and *perfect*

gift is from

above

James 1:17

Today, I Turn Over To God....

I Am Joyful Because....

My Future Includes....

I Will Practice More Self-Care By....

I Am...

Don't be
afraid
just
Believe

•Mark 5:36•

I Know God Cares Because....

Father, Forgive Me For....

My Life Is Meaningful Because....

I Have Peace & Contentment About....

I Am Blessed Because....

Be **strong**
Be **brave**
Be **fearless**

You are never alone

• Joshua 1:9 •

I Am In Awe Of....

My Hope for Tomorrow Is....

Thank You Father, For....

I Will Keep My Thoughts Focused On....

God, Please Use Me To....

Forgive

one another

just as

GOD

Forgave

you

Ephesians 4:32

In All Things, God Help Me Remember That....

Nothing Is Impossible Because....

I Will Spread Love By....

God, Grant Me The Serenity To....

Thank You God For Showing Me....

I can do all things through Christ who strengthens me

Philippians 4:13

I Let Go Of Past Negative Beliefs About....

I Love....

God, Please Help Me To....

God, Thank You For Your Mercy In....

I Declare....

Loved

Romans 5:8

I Wish To Experience More....

I Dream That I....

I Feel Closer To God When I....

I Pray....

I Accept....

WHEN YOU GO THROUGH DEEP WATERS

I will be with you

Isaiah 43:2

In This Season Of Change, I Humbly Ask For...

God, Please Hold My Hand Through....

I Have the Power In Me To....

I Am Excited About....

I Give Praise For....

With his

love

he will calm

all your

fears

• Zephaniah 3:17 •

God, I Believe That You Will....

God, Thank You For....

Lord, Please Make Plain To Me....

I Pray For Peace About....

God, Please Hear My Prayer For....

Love
ANCHORS
THE Soul
<Hebrews 6:19>

I Celebrate....

For My Family, I Pray...

I Choose Peace In....

I Hope That....

I Pray for My Relationship With....

Let your light shine

Matthew 5:16

God, I Just Want To Thank You For....

I No Longer Cry About...

I Now Know....

My Thoughts Are Renewed About....

I Believe....

Thank You God for Inner Guidance About...

I Can Achieve Anything Because...

AS FOR ME
AND
MY HOUSE
WE WILL
SERVE THE
Lord

Joshua 24:15

Made in United States
Orlando, FL
15 December 2024

55732710R00055